2021 Alaska Outdoor Photos Calendar

(Full Moon Dates = ☺)

Copyright © 2020 Daniel H. Wieczorek & Kazuya Numazawa

ISBN-13: 979-8-6983-0021-2

PHOTOS INCLUDED IN THIS CALENDAR

January: The January moon prepares to set behind the hills north of Fairbanks, Alaska.

February: Is it rime, hoar frost, or something else? Some kind of ice on the vegetation at Murphy Dome, near Fairbanks, Alaska.

March: Bohemian Waxwings (*Bombycilla garrulous*) stop by for some chokecherries near Fairbanks, Alaska.

April: Pasque Flowers (*Pulsatilla patens*) celebrate the first warm days of spring near Fairbanks, Alaska.

May: Gorman's Dwarf Primrose (*Douglasia gormanii*) on a mountainside near Healy, Alaska.

June: Frigid Shooting-Star (*Dodecatheon frigidum*) near Eagle Summit, Alaska.

July: Chocolate Lily (*Fritillaria camschatcensis*) near Willow, Alaska.

August: Northern Lady-Slipper Orchid (*Cypripedium passerinum*) near Central, Alaska.

September: Fireleaf Leptarrhena (*Leptarrhena pyrolifolia*) near Willow, Alaska.

October: Late autumn colors near Nome Creek, Chatanika, Alaska.

November: Sunrise through the birch-aspen forest on an overcast morning near Fairbanks, Alaska.

December: Snow-covered mountains near Eagle Summit, Alaska.

The January moon prepares to set behind the hills north of Fairbanks, Alaska.

January 2021

Sun	Mon	Tue	Wed	Thu	Fri	Sat
27	28	29	30	31	1 New Year's Day	2
3	4	5	6	7	8	9
10	11	12	13	14	15	16
17	18 Martin Luther King Jr. Day	19	20	21	22	23
24	25	26	27	☺	29	30
31	1	2	3	4	5	6

Is it rime, hoar frost, or something else? Some kind of ice on the vegetation at Murphy Dome, near Fairbanks, Alaska.

February 2021

Sun	Mon	Tue	Wed	Thu	Fri	Sat
31	1	2	3	4	5	6
7	8	9	10	11	12	13
14 Valentine's Day	15 President's Day	16	17	18	19	20
21	22	23	24	25	26	
28	1	2	3	4	5	6

Bohemian Waxwings (*Bombycilla garrulous*) stop by for some chokecherries near Fairbanks, Alaska.

March 2021

Sun	Mon	Tue	Wed	Thu	Fri	Sat
28	1	2	3	4	5	6
7	8	9	10	11	12	13
14 Daylight Saving Time Begin (02:00)	15	16	17 St. Patrick's Day	18	19	20 09:37 GMT Vernal Equinox
21	22	23	24	25	26	27
	29	30	31	1	2	3

Pasque Flowers (*Pulsatilla patens*) celebrate the first warm days of spring near Fairbanks, Alaska.

<table>
<tr><th>April</th><th colspan="6"></th><th>2021</th></tr>
<tr><th>Sun</th><th>Mon</th><th>Tue</th><th>Wed</th><th>Thu</th><th>Fri</th><th>Sat</th></tr>
<tr><td>28</td><td>29</td><td>30</td><td>31</td><td>1</td><td>2</td><td>3</td></tr>
<tr><td>4
Easter Sunday</td><td>5</td><td>6</td><td>7</td><td>8</td><td>9</td><td>10</td></tr>
<tr><td>11</td><td>12</td><td>13</td><td>14</td><td>15</td><td>16</td><td>17</td></tr>
<tr><td>18</td><td>19</td><td>20</td><td>21</td><td>22</td><td>23</td><td>24</td></tr>
<tr><td>25</td><td>☺</td><td>27</td><td>28</td><td>29</td><td>30</td><td>1</td></tr>
</table>

Gorman's Dwarf Primrose (*Douglasia gormanii*) on a mountainside near Healy, Alaska.

May 2021

Sun	Mon	Tue	Wed	Thu	Fri	Sat
25	26	27	28	29	30	1
2	3	4	5	6	7	8
9 Mother's Day	10	11	12	13	14	15
16	17	18	19	20	21	22
23	24	25	😇	27	28	29
30	31 Memorial Day	1	2	3	4	5

Frigid Shooting-Star (*Dodecatheon frigidum*) near Eagle Summit, Alaska.

June 2021

Sun	Mon	Tue	Wed	Thu	Fri	Sat
30	31	1	2	3	4	5
6	7	8	9	10	11	12
13	14	15	16	17	18	19 03:32 GMT Summer Solstice
20 Father's Day	21	22	23	🌚	25	26
27	28	29	30	1	2	3

Chocolate Lily (*Fritillaria camschatcensis*) near Willow, Alaska.

July 2021

Sun	Mon	Tue	Wed	Thu	Fri	Sat
27	28	29	30	1	2	3
4 Independence Day	5 Independence Day (Observed)	6	7	8	9	10
11	12	13	14	15	16	17
18	19	20	21	22	☺	24
25	26	27	28	29	30	31

Northern Lady-Slipper Orchid (*Cypripedium passerinum*) near Central, Alaska.

Sun	Mon	Tue	Wed	Thu	Fri	Sat
1	2	3	4	5	6	7
8	9	10	11	12	13	14
15	16	17	18	19	20	21
	23	24	25	26	27	28
29	30	31	1	2	3	4

Fireleaf Leptarrhena (*Leptarrhena pyrolifolia*) near Willow, Alaska.

Sun	Mon	Tue	Wed	Thu	Fri	Sat
29	30	31	1	2	3	4
5	6 Labor Day	7	8	9	10	11
12	13	14	15	16	17	18
19	20	21	22 19:21 GMT Autumnal Equinox	23	24	25
26	27	28	29	30	1	2

Late autumn colors near Nome Creek, Chatanika, Alaska.

October 2021

Sun	Mon	Tue	Wed	Thu	Fri	Sat
26	27	28	29	30	1	2
3	4	5	6	7	8	9
10	11 Columbus Day	12	13	14	15	16
17	18	19	🌝	21	22	23
24	25	26	27	28	29	30
31 Halloween	1	2	3	4	5	6

Sunrise through the birch-aspen forest on an overcast morning near Fairbanks, Alaska.

November 2021

Sun	Mon	Tue	Wed	Thu	Fri	Sat
31	1	2	3	4	5	6
7 **Daylight Saving Time End (02:00)**	8	9	10	11 **Veteran's Day**	12	13
14	15	16	17	18		20
21	22	23	24	25 **Thanksgiving Day**	26	27
28	29	30	1	2	3	4

Snow-covered mountains near Eagle Summit, Alaska.

December 2021

Sun	Mon	Tue	Wed	Thu	Fri	Sat
28	29	30	1	2	3	4
5	6	7	8	9	10	11
12	13	14	15	16	17	
19	20	21 03:59 GMT Winter Solstice	22	23	24 Christmas Eve	25 Christmas Day
26	27	28	29	30	31 New Year's Day (Observed)	1

2021 Phases of the Moon

Universal Time (GMT)

	New Moon				First Quarter				Full Moon				Last Quarter		
	d	h	m		d	h	m		d	h	m		d	h	m
—	—	—	—	—	—	—	—	—	—	—	—	JAN	06	09	37
JAN	13	05	00	JAN	20	21	01	JAN	28	19	16	FEB	04	17	37
FEB	11	19	05	FEB	19	18	47	FEB	27	08	17	MAR	06	01	30
MAR	13	10	21	MAR	21	15	40	MAR	28	19	48	APR	04	11	02
APR	12	03	30	APR	20	07	58	APR	27	04	31	MAY	03	20	50
MAY	11	19	59	MAY	19	20	12	MAY	26	12	13	JUN	02	08	24
JUN	10	11	52	JUN	18	04	54	JUN	24	19	39	JUL	01	22	10
JUL	10	02	16	JUL	17	11	10	JUL	24	03	36	JUL	31	14	15
AUG	08	14	50	AUG	15	16	19	AUG	22	13	01	AUG	30	08	13
SEP	07	01	51	SEP	13	21	39	SEP	20	00	54	SEP	29	02	57
OCT	06	12	05	OCT	13	04	25	OCT	20	15	56	OCT	28	21	05
NOV	04	22	14	NOV	11	12	45	NOV	19	08	57	NOV	27	12	27
DEC	04	07	43	DEC	11	01	35	DEC	19	04	35	DEC	27	02	23

Earth's Seasons – 2021

Universal Time (GMT)

		d	h				d	h	m		d	h	m
Perihelion	Jan	21	08	Equinoxes	Mar	20	09	37	Sept	22	19	21
Aphelion	July	05	06	Solstices	June	19	03	32	Dec	21	03	59

If you enjoyed the photographs shown in this calendar then please be sure to check out our website. It can be found at http://danwiz.com. As long as Daniel is alive he hopes to be able to maintain it.

Kazuya's Photos: **February.**
Daniel's Photos: **January, March, April, May, June, July, August, September, October, November, December.**